Solitary Sudoku

New Number and Logic Puzzles

How it all began

In May 2000 I had an accident, falling from a ladder, and needed 5 months off work.

Boredom soon set in and as I love numbers I decided to try and devise some number puzzles.

I put three rows of numbers from 1 to 9 on a spreadsheet. I then inserted a formula that added the middle number to the top and bottom numbers and printed out the result.

I then erased all the numbers just leaving the top and bottom totals then by using addition tried to reinstate the correct numbers.

It was then that I had that "Eureka" moment, realising that because the middle row was common to both sums, up and down, it would need logic to place the correct combinations in the right order, and so my ZYGO puzzle was born!

I had a new addictive hobby.

In the years that followed I devised many new number puzzles and compiled computer programs that generated them automatically.

A year or two ago, I thought I would try and get some puzzles published and contacted Andrew Griffin at Tarquin who decided to publish 6 puzzle books for everyone to enjoy.

Solitary Sudoku

New Number and Logic Puzzles

Les Page

Tarquin

Publisher's Note

If you have enjoyed this Solitary Sudoku book and want a further challenge there are 5 other books in the series - as you can see opposite. - fuller details on www.tarquingroup.com. Enjoy!

Try before you Buy
You can try some puzzles from the other books at the back of this book. Bonus puzzles start at page 55.

Les Page has asserted his right to be identified as the author of this work under the Copyright, Designs and Patents Act 1988.

© Les Page 2020

ISBN UK (Book) 978-1-913565-04-6

ISBN (EBook) 978-1-913565-05-3

Designed and Printed in the UK

Tarquin

Suite 74, 17 Holywell Hill

St Albans AL1 1DT

UK

www.tarquingroup.com

Solitary Sudoku

Contents

Puzzles 1–26

Start on page 1 overleaf. Solutions to each are on reverse side of the puzzle page.

Emojis -
Tougher puzzles
Book ISBN 9781913565008
Ebook ISBN 9781913565015

Nightmare Blocks
Book ISBN 9781913565022
Ebook ISBN 9781913565039

The Compendium
Book ISBN 9781913565060
Ebook ISBN 9781913565077

Starter Puzzles

Emojis -
The Starter Book
Book ISBN 9781913565084
Ebook ISBN 9781913565091

Nightmare Blocks -
The Starter Book
Book ISBN 9781913565107
Ebook ISBN 9781913565114

SOLITARY SUDOKU

SOLITARY SUDOKU

A different slant on the Sudoku puzzle ...
by looking for solitary numbers.

By checking for SOLITARY numbers (i.e. numbers that appear on their own, just once, in any ROW and COLUMN and once in each of the nine 3 x 3 grids) and blocking out unwanted "option" numbers, certain Sudoku puzzles can be solved.

The SOLITARY SUDOKU puzzle in this book allows you to do that.

Please see the Rules/Instructions set out on the next 2 pages.

© Les Page 2020   ISBN 9781913565046   For more www.tarquingroup.com

SOLITARY SUDOKU

Rules/Instructions

The Solitary Sudoku puzzle contains all the options that could apply for solving the puzzle.

The options appear in ROWS that contain numbers:

1	2	3		4	5	6	and	7	8	9

and in COLUMNS that contain numbers:

1	2		3
4	5	and	6
7	8		9

Solitary numbers are defined as numbers that appear on their own, just once, in any ROW and COLUMN and in each of the nine 3 x 3 grids.

INSTRUCTIONS:

(A) Look for "Solitary" numbers in a box on its own.
When one is found take the actions at (1), (2) & (3)

(B) Look for "Solitary" numbers across ROWS and COLUMNS.
When one is found take the actions at (1), (2) & (3)

(C) Look for "Solitary" numbers that appear in the nine 3 x 3 grids.
When one is found take the actions at (1), (2) & (3)

© Les Page 2020   ISBN 9781913565046   For more www.tarquingroup.com

SOLITARY SUDOKU

(1) Put a "circle" round the "Solitary" number found and "block out" all the other numbers in that box.

(2) Also "block out" the same number in the same ROW and COLUMN leading from it in all directions left & right and up & down.

(3) If there are any more of the same number in its 3 x 3 grid then block them out too.

Blocking out unwanted numbers will eventually create more "Solitary" numbers and sometimes chain reactions can occur which are very helpful.

It is good practise to tick each completed line when 1, 2, 3   4, 5, 6 and 7, 8, 9 are found and circled.

Good practise after finding a "Solitary" number is to have a fixed routine of checking up & down, side to side and then the 3 x 3 grid for blocking out unwanted numbers. That way, hopefully, none are missed being blocked out!

Remember the grid changes every time numbers are blocked out so it is vital that you keep on searching for "Solitary" numbers by looking down COLUMNS, across ROWS and within 3 x 3 grids until solved. Never give up!

If 5 was "Solitary" the grid would look like this after blocking out:

Solution 1 on page 10 should be very helpful as it is a full blocked out and circled solution. Other answers are given as a grid of solitary numbers only.

For more www.tarquingroup.com

SOLITARY SUDOKU

SOLITARY SUDOKU
LET'S LOOK AT PUZZLE 1 OPPOSITE

Here is some help to get you started on solving this puzzle:
There is a Solitary 8 in the box relating to ROW twelve from the top and 14 COLUMNS from the left (arrowed). It's all on its own in that box so circle it.

You must now "block out" the two 8's in the same ROW and also block out the four 8's in the same COLUMN below it.

You will see by blocking out the 8 in the ROW to the left of the Solitary 8 found that the number 5 that remains becomes a Solitary number too, so you must circle it.

There are two 5's to the right in the same ROW so you can block them out. There is also a 5 above in the same COLUMN so block that out and two more 5's below it which can be blocked out too.

There are also three more 5's in the same 3 x 3 grid so it is important to block them out as well.

A chain reaction has occurred and you will see that by blocking out a further Solitary number 3 has been created in ROW ten on the far right. You must circle that and block out the two 3's below it in the same COLUMN.

You can also tick that row as completed as 1, 2 & 3 have all been circled.

I hope this has demonstrated how to solve Solitary Sudoku.

Good Luck ! Les Page.

© Les Page 2020   ISBN 9781913565046   For more www.tarquingroup.com

SOLITARY SUDOKU

PUZZLE 1

Solution Overleaf

For more www.tarquingroup.com

SOLITARY SUDOKU

THIS IS THE CIRCLED & BLOCKED OUT SOLUTION TO PUZZLE 1

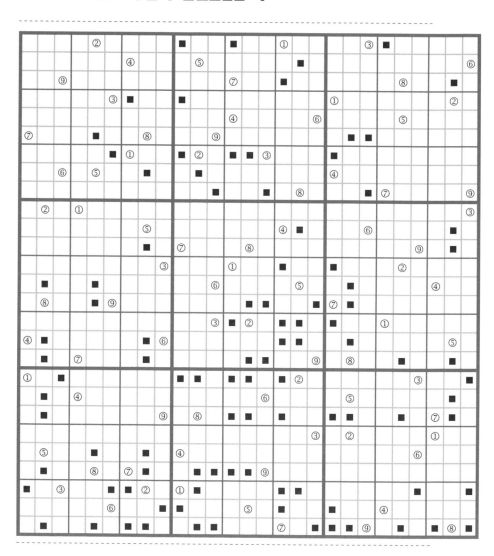

 ISBN 9781913565046   For more www.tarquingroup.com

SOLITARY SUDOKU

PUZZLE 2

© Les Page 2020   ISBN 9781913565046   For more www.tarquingroup.com

SOLUTION TO PUZZLE 2

8	1	9	4	5	3	7	2	6
3	4	6	2	1	7	9	5	8
5	7	2	8	6	9	1	3	4
4	5	8	6	9	2	3	1	7
6	2	7	1	3	5	4	8	9
1	9	3	7	4	8	5	6	2
7	3	1	9	8	6	2	4	5
9	8	5	3	2	4	6	7	1
2	6	4	5	7	1	8	9	3

PUZZLE 3

Solution Overleaf

For more www.tarquingroup.com

SOLUTION TO PUZZLE 3

3	2	1	5	4	8	9	6	7
4	9	6	7	3	1	8	5	2
7	8	5	9	6	2	4	1	3
6	4	2	1	7	9	3	8	5
8	3	7	4	5	6	2	9	1
5	1	9	8	2	3	7	4	6
1	7	8	3	9	5	6	2	4
9	6	4	2	1	7	5	3	8
2	5	3	6	8	4	1	7	9

SOLITARY SUDOKU

PUZZLE 4

Solution Overleaf

For more www.tarquingroup.com

SOLUTION TO PUZZLE 4

5	9	3	1	4	8	7	2	6
1	8	6	3	2	7	9	5	4
2	4	7	6	9	5	1	3	8
7	5	2	9	6	4	8	1	3
9	3	8	7	1	2	6	4	5
4	6	1	8	5	3	2	7	9
3	7	5	2	8	9	4	6	1
6	2	9	4	3	1	5	8	7
8	1	4	5	7	6	3	9	2

© Les Page 2020   ISBN 9781913565046

SOLITARY SUDOKU

PUZZLE 5

Solution Overleaf

© Les Page 2020   ISBN 9781913565046   For more www.tarquingroup.com

SOLUTION TO PUZZLE 5

5	9	2	6	8	1	7	3	4
4	6	3	7	5	2	9	1	8
8	7	1	4	3	9	6	2	5
1	3	8	2	6	5	4	7	9
6	2	5	9	4	7	1	8	3
9	4	7	8	1	3	5	6	2
7	5	9	1	2	8	3	4	6
2	1	4	3	9	6	8	5	7
3	8	6	5	7	4	2	9	1

                                   For more www.tarquingroup.com

SOLITARY SUDOKU

PUZZLE 6

Solution Overleaf

For more www.tarquingroup.com

SOLUTION TO PUZZLE 6

3	8	7	2	5	9	6	1	4
2	9	1	4	6	7	3	8	5
5	6	4	3	1	8	2	9	7
1	3	2	7	9	5	8	4	6
7	4	6	8	2	1	5	3	9
9	5	8	6	3	4	7	2	1
4	2	5	9	7	3	1	6	8
8	7	3	1	4	6	9	5	2
6	1	9	5	8	2	4	7	3

SOLITARY SUDOKU

PUZZLE 7

Solution Overleaf

For more www.tarquingroup.com

SOLUTION TO PUZZLE 7

8	3	7	6	1	9	5	2	4
2	9	1	5	3	4	7	8	6
4	6	5	7	2	8	9	3	1
6	2	9	3	4	1	8	5	7
1	5	8	2	9	7	6	4	3
7	4	3	8	5	6	1	9	2
5	7	4	1	8	3	2	6	9
3	8	6	9	7	2	4	1	5
9	1	2	4	6	5	3	7	8

SOLITARY SUDOKU

PUZZLE 8

1 2 4 5 7	2 5 7	3	1 2 5 7 8	1 2 5 8	6	5 7	9	5 8
1 5 6 7	5 6 7	9	1 5 7 8	1 5 8	1 3 5 7	4	3 5 6 7 8	2
2 5 6 7	2 5 6 7	8	4	2 5 9	2 3 5 7	1	3 5 6 7	3 5 6
1 2 5 8 9	4	1 2 5	3	6	1 2 5 7	5 7 9	1 5 7 8	1 5 8 9
1 3 5 6 8	3 5 6 8	1 5	1 5 7	1 5	9	2	4	1 3 5 6 8
1 2 3 5 6 9	2 3 5 6 9	7	1 2 5	1 2 4 5	8	3 5 9	1 3 5 6	1 3 5 6 9
2 4 5 8 9	1	2 4 5	2 5 6 8 9	3	2 4 5	5 9	5	7
3 4 5 7 8 9	3 5 7 8 9	4 5	1 5 8 9	1 4 5 8 9	1 4 5	6	2	1 3 5 9
2 3 5 9	2 3 5 9	6	1 2 5 9	7	1 2 5	8	1 3 5	4

Solution Overleaf

 ISBN 9781913565046

For more www.tarquingroup.com

SOLUTION TO PUZZLE 8

4	7	3	1	2	6	5	9	8
1	6	9	8	5	3	4	7	2
2	5	8	4	9	7	1	6	3
9	4	1	3	6	2	7	8	5
3	8	5	7	1	9	2	4	6
6	2	7	5	4	8	3	1	9
8	1	2	6	3	4	9	5	7
7	3	4	9	8	5	6	2	1
5	9	6	2	7	1	8	3	4

SOLITARY SUDOKU

PUZZLE 9

Solution Overleaf

© Les Page 2020   ISBN 9781913565046   For more www.tarquingroup.com

SOLUTION TO PUZZLE 9

2	4	3	7	5	6	9	1	8
6	9	8	4	1	3	5	2	7
7	1	5	8	9	2	4	3	6
8	7	1	6	4	5	2	9	3
9	5	6	2	3	7	8	4	1
3	2	4	1	8	9	6	7	5
4	8	9	3	6	1	7	5	2
5	3	7	9	2	8	1	6	4
1	6	2	5	7	4	3	8	9

SOLITARY SUDOKU

PUZZLE 10

Solution Overleaf

For more www.tarquingroup.com

SOLUTION TO PUZZLE 10

9	3	8	6	2	5	7	4	1
1	6	2	3	4	7	9	8	5
4	7	5	1	9	8	2	3	6
2	1	9	7	8	6	4	5	3
6	4	3	2	5	9	1	7	8
8	5	7	4	1	3	6	2	9
5	8	6	9	7	2	3	1	4
7	9	4	5	3	1	8	6	2
3	2	1	8	6	4	5	9	7

SOLITARY SUDOKU

PUZZLE 11

1			3							1		2	1		
			4			6		6	5						6
	8	9			7	9	7				7	8		8	
		1	2	1	2			3	1				1		
	5		6		6	6			4			4	6		6
				7	7				7		9	7	8	8	
1		1		1	2							3		1	
		6			6		4	6				4	5	6	6
	9		9	7			7			8		7			
				2	3		1			3					3
	6				5						4		9		
			8						7				9		
		1		1	3				3		2	3			
					4			6				6		5	
7			9					8					8		
	3				3		3					1	2		
4			5				6				4				
						8		9				8	7		
	2	3		2	1			2					3	2	3
4		4					4		6	5		5	5		
					9		7	8			7	8	7	8	8
1	2	3	1	2			3			3	1		3		
			6					5	5					4	
				8	7		9		7	9	7	7			
1	2	3		1	2	3	3		2	3		3	1	2	3
4				5			4		4			6	5		
		7				8	9		8	9			8	8	9

Solution Overleaf

For more www.tarquingroup.com

SOLUTION TO PUZZLE 11

8	3	4	9	6	5	7	2	1
5	2	6	7	3	1	9	4	8
9	1	7	2	4	8	3	5	6
6	8	2	5	1	7	4	9	3
7	9	1	4	8	3	2	6	5
4	5	3	6	9	2	8	1	7
3	4	9	1	7	6	5	8	2
2	6	8	3	5	9	1	7	4
1	7	5	8	2	4	6	3	9

 ISBN 9781913565046

SOLITARY SUDOKU

PUZZLE 12

Solution Overleaf

© Les Page 2020   ISBN 9781913565046

For more www.tarquingroup.com

SOLUTION TO PUZZLE 12

4	3	8	9	7	6	2	1	5
5	9	2	3	4	1	8	7	6
7	1	6	8	5	2	9	4	3
3	5	7	2	6	8	1	9	4
8	2	4	5	1	9	6	3	7
1	6	9	4	3	7	5	8	2
2	8	3	6	9	4	7	5	1
6	4	1	7	8	5	3	2	9
9	7	5	1	2	3	4	6	8

SOLITARY SUDOKU

PUZZLE 13

© Les Page 2020   ISBN 9781913565046   For more www.tarquingroup.com

SOLUTION TO PUZZLE 13

7	3	9	2	4	1	8	6	5
5	2	4	6	9	8	3	1	7
8	6	1	3	5	7	4	2	9
2	5	6	8	7	3	1	9	4
4	8	3	9	1	5	6	7	2
1	9	7	4	6	2	5	8	3
9	4	2	5	8	6	7	3	1
3	1	8	7	2	4	9	5	6
6	7	5	1	3	9	2	4	8

SOLITARY SUDOKU

PUZZLE 14

Solution Overleaf

For more www.tarquingroup.com

SOLUTION TO PUZZLE 14

9	5	2	8	3	4	6	1	7
7	8	3	1	2	6	5	4	9
6	1	4	5	7	9	3	8	2
8	7	1	6	9	5	4	2	3
3	6	5	2	4	7	1	9	8
4	2	9	3	1	8	7	6	5
2	3	8	7	6	1	9	5	4
5	4	6	9	8	3	2	7	1
1	9	7	4	5	2	8	3	6

For more www.tarquingroup.com

PUZZLE 15

Solution Overleaf

For more www.tarquingroup.com

SOLUTION TO PUZZLE 15

3	4	8	2	9	1	7	6	5
1	2	5	6	4	7	8	9	3
9	7	6	3	5	8	4	1	2
2	9	3	5	8	6	1	4	7
5	6	7	4	1	9	2	3	8
4	8	1	7	2	3	9	5	6
7	1	4	8	3	5	6	2	9
8	3	9	1	6	2	5	7	4
6	5	2	9	7	4	3	8	1

PUZZLE 16

Solution Overleaf

For more www.tarquingroup.com

SOLUTION TO PUZZLE 16

4	5	9	7	2	1	3	6	8
8	7	3	5	4	6	9	2	1
2	6	1	9	8	3	7	4	5
5	8	2	3	1	9	6	7	4
9	3	4	8	6	7	1	5	2
6	1	7	4	5	2	8	9	3
3	9	5	1	7	4	2	8	6
1	4	6	2	9	8	5	3	7
7	2	8	6	3	5	4	1	9

SOLITARY SUDOKU

PUZZLE 17

Solution Overleaf

For more www.tarquingroup.com

SOLUTION TO PUZZLE 17

8	5	3	2	4	1	9	7	6
7	1	6	3	8	9	5	2	4
2	4	9	6	7	5	1	8	3
1	3	8	4	5	6	7	9	2
5	9	7	8	2	3	4	6	1
4	6	2	1	9	7	3	5	8
9	2	1	5	3	8	6	4	7
6	8	5	7	1	4	2	3	9
3	7	4	9	6	2	8	1	5

SOLITARY SUDOKU

PUZZLE 18

For more www.tarquingroup.com

SOLUTION TO PUZZLE 18

1	7	3	8	6	9	2	5	4
4	6	9	1	5	2	3	7	8
8	2	5	3	7	4	9	1	6
3	8	6	5	9	1	4	2	7
7	5	4	2	3	6	8	9	1
9	1	2	7	4	8	5	6	3
5	4	8	9	1	7	6	3	2
6	3	1	4	2	5	7	8	9
2	9	7	6	8	3	1	4	5

SOLITARY SUDOKU

PUZZLE 19

Solution Overleaf

For more www.tarquingroup.com

SOLUTION TO PUZZLE 19

5	6	7	9	2	3	4	1	8
9	2	8	1	5	4	3	6	7
1	3	4	7	8	6	2	9	5
6	7	2	8	4	5	9	3	1
8	1	9	2	3	7	5	4	6
4	5	3	6	9	1	8	7	2
2	9	6	4	7	8	1	5	3
3	4	1	5	6	2	7	8	9
7	8	5	3	1	9	6	2	4

© Les Page 2020   ISBN 9781913565046

SOLITARY SUDOKU

PUZZLE 20

© Les Page 2020   ISBN 9781913565046

For more www.tarquingroup.com

SOLUTION TO PUZZLE 20

1	8	9	3	2	5	4	7	6
7	5	2	6	8	4	1	3	9
3	4	6	1	9	7	2	8	5
9	1	8	4	6	2	7	5	3
4	3	7	5	1	9	6	2	8
2	6	5	8	7	3	9	1	4
6	2	1	9	5	8	3	4	7
5	7	4	2	3	6	8	9	1
8	9	3	7	4	1	5	6	2

     For more www.tarquingroup.com

PUZZLE 21

Solution Overleaf

For more www.tarquingroup.com

SOLUTION TO PUZZLE 21

6	4	2	8	7	5	3	1	9
5	3	1	9	6	2	4	8	7
7	9	8	3	1	4	5	6	2
9	5	7	6	3	8	1	2	4
3	8	4	5	2	1	9	7	6
2	1	6	7	4	9	8	5	3
1	2	9	4	8	6	7	3	5
4	6	3	1	5	7	2	9	8
8	7	5	2	9	3	6	4	1

 ISBN 9781913565046   For more www.tarquingroup.com

SOLITARY SUDOKU

PUZZLE 22

Solution Overleaf

For more www.tarquingroup.com

SOLUTION TO PUZZLE 22

1	2	9	7	3	5	8	6	4
7	5	6	4	8	9	1	2	3
3	8	4	1	6	2	7	5	9
6	1	7	9	5	3	2	4	8
9	4	8	2	7	6	3	1	5
5	3	2	8	1	4	9	7	6
4	7	3	5	9	1	6	8	2
2	9	1	6	4	8	5	3	7
8	6	5	3	2	7	4	9	1

SOLITARY SUDOKU

PUZZLE 23

Solution Overleaf

For more www.tarquingroup.com

SOLUTION TO PUZZLE 23

6	9	5	8	3	4	7	2	1
1	7	2	9	5	6	8	3	4
4	3	8	1	2	7	9	5	6
9	6	4	7	1	5	2	8	3
7	2	1	4	8	3	6	9	5
5	8	3	6	9	2	4	1	7
2	1	7	3	6	8	5	4	9
3	5	6	2	4	9	1	7	8
8	4	9	5	7	1	3	6	2

© Les Page 2020   ISBN 9781913565046

15 EMOJIS have different numerical values. Put the values in the puzzle grid to agree the sum totals horizontally, vertically and diagonally.

Cross out numerical values when placed

↓ = ∩ Enter values when worked out   Yellow boxes are "given" values

1 x	👆	=	
2 x	😐	=	4
1 x	👉	=	
2 x	❖	=	
2 x	✈	=	
2 x	✋	=	21
2 x	☹	=	13
2 x	☺	=	16
1 x	👍	=	
2 x	💣	=	
2 x	⌘	=	
1 x	☝	=	
2 x	🏳	=	6
1 x	👎	=	
2 x	☠	=	9

↘	↓	↓	↓	↓	↓	↙
→	😐	⌘	👆	✋	🏳	65
→	👎	🏳	👍	☠	☠	39
→	👉	✈	☺	☹	❖	71
→	✋	😐	💣	☹	☝	43
→	💣	☺	✈	⌘	❖	76
38	40	64	59	76	55	58

↘	↓	↓	↓	↓	↓	↙
→	4			21	6	65
→		6		9	9	39
→			16	13		71
→	21	4		13		43
→		16				76
38	40	64	59	76	55	58

Cross out
2
3
4
5
6
7
8
9
13
14
16
18
19
20
21

Solution Overleaf

PUZZLE PREVIEW EMOJIS STARTER

SOLUTION

↘	↓	↓	↓	↓	↓	↙
→	☺	⌘	☞	✋	⚑	65
→	👎	⚑	👍	☠	☠	39
→	☞	✈	☺	☹	❖	71
→	✋	☺	💣	☹	☝	43
→	💣	☺	✈	⌘	❖	76
38	40	64	59	76	55	58

↘	↓	↓	↓	↓	↓	↙
→	4	20	14	21	6	65
→	7	6	8	9	9	39
→	5	18	16	13	19	71
→	21	4	3	13	2	43
→	3	16	18	20	19	76
38	40	64	59	76	55	58

☝	=	2
💣	=	3
☺	=	4
☞	=	5
⚑	=	6
👎	=	7
👍	=	8
☠	=	9
☹	=	13
☞	=	14
☺	=	16
✈	=	18
❖	=	19
⌘	=	20
✋	=	21

PUZZLE

WHAT'S IN STORE HERE ?

A warehouse has 25 large rooms. Each room has six storage areas numbered from 1 to 6. Each room has interlinking glass doors to other rooms. The storage areas adjacent to the interlinking glass doors have the same storage area number as shown in the example below:

6	or	4	4
6		↖	↗

interlinking glass doors

Insert the missing storage area numbers so that each room contains storage area numbers 1 to 6.

3	5	1
1	5	2
4	3	6
5	3	2

C1	C2	C3	C4	C5	C6	C7	C8
			4		5		
3	5		6	3	2	3	1
			1		4		
1							3
5			3			1	5
4							6
1		5				3	5
6							4
2			4			5	3
3							1
4		2			6		5
2			3				2
6		5				1	6
1							1
5		6				5	4
6				3			
1			5		4	3	5
			1		2		

Solution Overleaf

SOLUTION

LOOK ! ↘ HAVING "DONE TIME" PROVES IT CAN BE SOLVED ! 👆 ☺

			4	1	5			
3	5	6	6	3	2	2	3	1
2	4	1	1	3	4	4	6	5
1	4	6	6	5	2	2	6	3
5	2	3	3	5	1	1	4	5
4	2	6	6	4	2	2	4	6
1	3	5	5	4	3	3	1	5
6	3	1	1	2	6	6	1	4
2	5	4	4	2	5	5	2	3
3	5	6	6	1	3	3	2	1
4	1	2	2	1	6	6	4	5
2	1	3	3	4	5	5	4	2
6	4	5	5	4	1	1	3	6
1	4	3	3	2	6	6	3	1
5	2	6	6	2	5	5	2	4
6	2	4	4	3	1	1	2	6
1	3	5	5	3	4	4	3	5
			1	6	2			

The 15 letters in **NIGHTMARE BLOCKS** have different numerical values. Place values to agree sum totals horizontally, vertically and diagonally.

Cross out numerical values when placed

↓ = ∩ Enter values when worked out   Green boxes are "given" values

2 x	**N**	=	15
2 x	**I**	=	
2 x	**G**	=	21
2 x	**H**	=	19
2 x	**T**	=	
2 x	**M**	=	
2 x	**A**	=	1
2 x	**R**	=	
2 x	**E**	=	
2 x	**B**	=	10
1 x	**L**	=	
1 x	**O**	=	
1 x	**C**	=	
1 x	**K**	=	
1 x	**S**	=	

↘	↓	↓	↓	↓	↓	↙
→	N	I	O	C	B	52
→	E	A	T	H	R	40
→	G	R	A	M	S	49
→	K	B	I	G	H	68
→	T	M	N	L	E	70
48	55	50	46	83	45	47

↘	↓	↓	↓	↓	↓	↙
→	15				10	52
→		1		19		40
→	21		1			49
→		10		21	19	68
→			15			70
48	55	50	46	83	45	47

Values
1
2
3
4
5
6
8
9
10
15
16
18
19
20
21

Solution Overleaf

SOLUTION

↘	↓	↓	↓	↓	↓	↙
→	N	I	O	C	B	52
→	E	A	T	H	R	40
→	G	R	A	M	S	49
→	K	B	I	G	H	68
→	T	M	N	L	E	70
48	55	50	46	83	45	47

↘	↓	↓	↓	↓	↓	↙
→	15	16	6	5	10	52
→	9	1	8	19	3	40
→	21	3	1	20	4	49
→	2	10	16	21	19	68
→	8	20	15	18	9	70
48	55	50	46	83	45	47

A	=	1
K	=	2
R	=	3
S	=	4
C	=	5
O	=	6
T	=	8
E	=	9
B	=	10
N	=	15
I	=	16
L	=	18
H	=	19
M	=	20
G	=	21

Scribble Page

Need a New Tarquin Challenge?

We have a series of number and logic puzzles for a variety of ages and skill levels. See all at our website - but here are a selection:

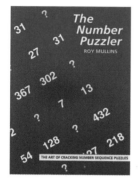

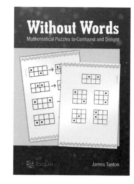

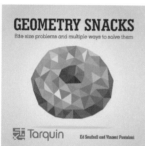

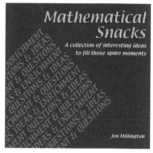

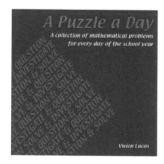

Bestselling titles like Without Words, Geometry Snacks and A Puzzle a Day will be joined by Birds, Bees and Burgers in 2021.

Buy Tarquin books in most trade outlets or from www.tarquingroup.com